the Country Friends® Collection

Trash to Treasure

Holly
...found a dollhouse just like her old one at an auction for $10.00.

Mary Elizabeth
...salvaged enough old-time homespun to quilt into a duvet cover.

Kate
...bought an autographed football, signed by King Louis IV.

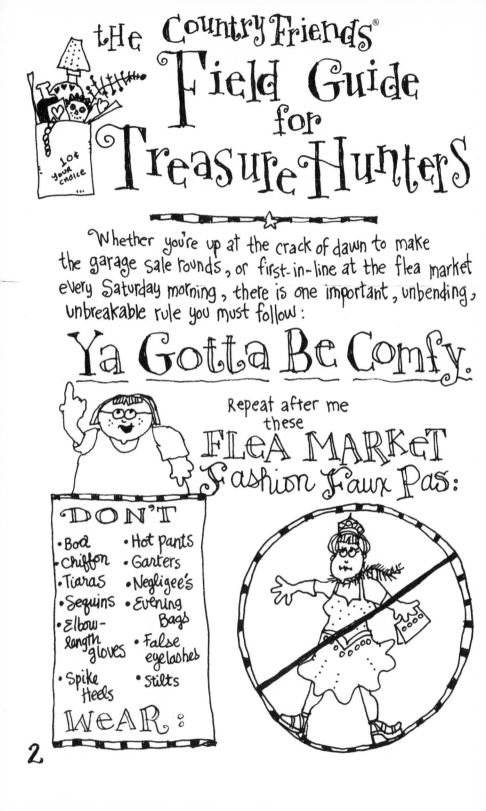

tHe Country Friends® Field Guide for Treasure Hunters

Whether you're up at the crack of dawn to make the garage sale rounds, or first-in-line at the flea market every Saturday morning, there is one important, unbending, unbreakable rule you must follow:

Ya Gotta Be Comfy.

Repeat after me these FLeA MARKeT Fashion Faux Pas:

DON'T

- Boa
- Chiffon
- Tiaras
- Sequins
- Elbow-length gloves
- Spike Heels
- Hot pants
- Garters
- Negligee's
- Evening Bags
- False eyelashes
- Stilts

WeAR:

Exhibit A: The Uniform

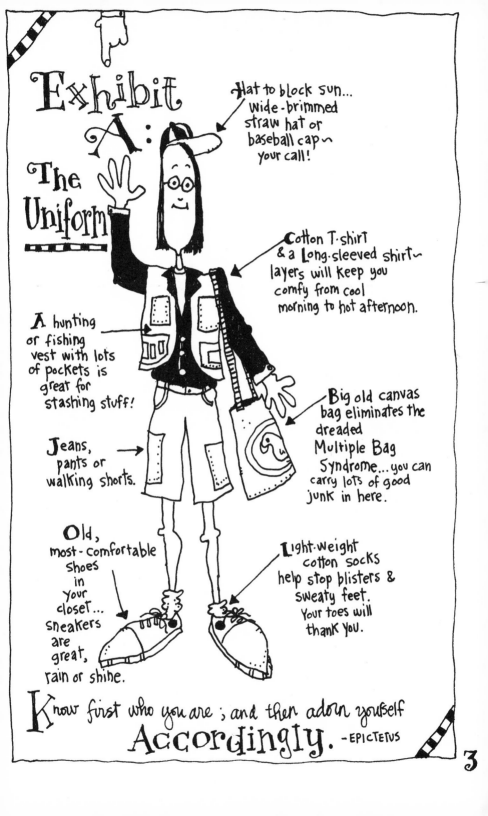

Hat to block sun... Wide-brimmed straw hat or baseball cap~ your call!

Cotton T-shirt & a Long-sleeved shirt~ layers will keep you comfy from cool morning to hot afternoon.

A hunting or fishing vest with lots of pockets is great for stashing stuff!

Jeans, pants or walking shorts.

Big old canvas bag eliminates the dreaded Multiple Bag Syndrome... you can carry lots of good junk in here.

Old, most-comfortable shoes in your closet... sneakers are great, rain or shine.

Light-weight cotton socks help stop blisters & sweaty feet. Your toes will thank you.

Know first who you are; and then adorn yourself **Accordingly.** —EPICTETUS

Field Guide (continued)

The experienced treasure hunter knows what kind of tools to carry:

Exhibit B: The Equipment

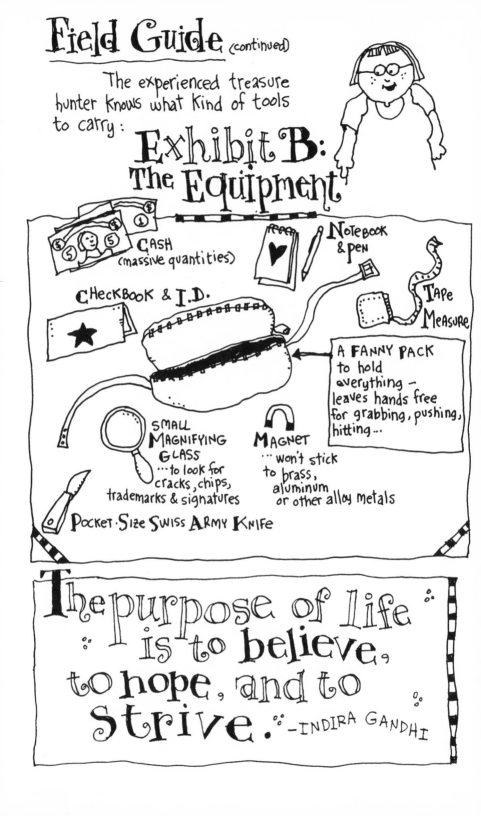

CASH (massive quantities)

NOTEBOOK & PEN

CHECKBOOK & I.D.

TAPE MEASURE

A **FANNY PACK** to hold everything – leaves hands free for grabbing, pushing, hitting...

SMALL MAGNIFYING GLASS ...to look for cracks, chips, trademarks & signatures

MAGNET ...won't stick to brass, aluminum or other alloy metals

POCKET·SIZE SWISS ARMY KNIFE

> The purpose of life is to believe, to hope, and to strive. –INDIRA GANDHI

Make like a girl scout and

Be Prepared.

You gotta have a game plan but in a spontaneous kind of way... get it? For example:

★ **M**ake a **L**ist and check it twice... it will help you stay focused on things you're looking for ...

...but just because that 6 foot·tall vintage stoplight isn't <u>on</u> that list doesn't necessarily mean you don't NEED it.

★ **B**udget your money; think about how much you're willing to pay <u>ahead</u> of time...

...but remember, too, that a person <u>can</u> survive for quite a long while on macaroni, soda crackers and tap water.

★ **P**ractice negotiating— it's part of the fun of shopping.

"What's your best price?" ... "How low can you go?"... are perfectly acceptable...

...but "I'll give you $25 plus this cute baby" is probably not a good idea.

5

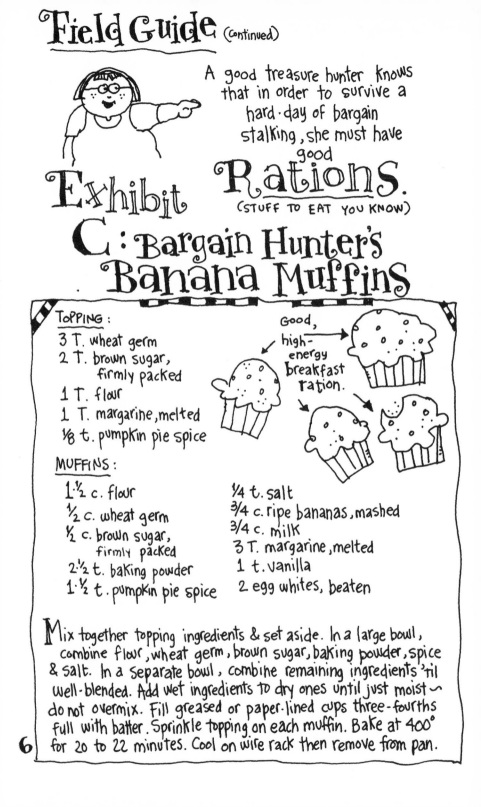

A good treasure hunter knows that in order to survive a hard-day of bargain stalking, she must have good **Rations.**

(STUFF TO EAT YOU KNOW)

Exhibit C: Bargain Hunter's Banana Muffins

TOPPING:

- 3 T. wheat germ
- 2 T. brown sugar, firmly packed
- 1 T. flour
- 1 T. margarine, melted
- ⅛ t. pumpkin pie spice

Good, high-energy breakfast ration.

MUFFINS:

- 1½ c. flour
- ½ c. wheat germ
- ½ c. brown sugar, firmly packed
- 2½ t. baking powder
- 1½ t. pumpkin pie spice
- ¼ t. salt
- ¾ c. ripe bananas, mashed
- ¾ c. milk
- 3 T. margarine, melted
- 1 t. vanilla
- 2 egg whites, beaten

Mix together topping ingredients & set aside. In a large bowl, combine flour, wheat germ, brown sugar, baking powder, spice & salt. In a separate bowl, combine remaining ingredients 'til well-blended. Add wet ingredients to dry ones until just moist — do not overmix. Fill greased or paper-lined cups three-fourths full with batter. Sprinkle topping on each muffin. Bake at 400° for 20 to 22 minutes. Cool on wire rack then remove from pan.

In treasure hunting, it's every man for himself. It pays to

KNOW Your Competition.

Learn to spot these typical shoppers in **Exhibit D:**

THE WAITING & WAVERING
YES·ER·NOERUS
... just can't decide whether to buy it or not... don't you wait-swoop in for the kill!

THE GREEN-BACKED **SHOPARIUS**
... money is no object. There's no point in trying to outbid this one. Move on.

THE **PUSHIN'-N-SHOVIN' PUGILISTICA**
... expert in shopping hand-to-hand combat. Not above elbowing her way to the front of the line. Don't get in her way at the next tag sale!

Things may come to those who wait, but only the things left by those who **hustle.** – Abraham Lincoln

SALE TODAY→

7

What to look for.

The list, of course, is endless but here are some of our favorites that are still affordable & fun:

Exhibit E:
Architectural Stuff

Old Windows

can be fitted with a mirror or simply hung on the wall.

*Add a window box to the frame for a unique arbor.

*Have a woodworking buddy build a shallow box behind your window frame for an inventive wall cupboard — perfect for small collections of other flea market stuff!

Shutters

... grungy old paint, four layers of peeling orange shellac... we love 'em! Hinge tall ones together for a folding screen... line 'em up behind your bed and tack them to the wall for an artful headboard... Accent a window on the *inside*... display small framed art & photos on a shutter — a country style bulletin board!

8

Fireplace Mantels

make a cozy accent in a room... even without the working fireplace behind it! Fill the opening with crocks & baskets full of seasonal flowers.

A mantel also serves as a wonderful headboard. Here's how:

1. Cut a piece of plywood about ¼" smaller on all sides than the mantel's opening.
2. Cover plywood with several layers of thick polyester batting. Fold edges of batting over the plywood and tack into place with a staple gun.
3. Finish with a piece of heavyweight upholstery-type fabric that is cut 5" longer on all sides than the plywood. Fold under raw edges ~ tack into place with staple gun or upholstery tacks. Pull fabric taut to prevent wrinkles in the finished project.

Porch Posts and Gingerbread

are positively FULL of personality! Build wonderful furniture from old posts... use a ⅞" drill bit to make a hole 1" deep in antique balusters for great looking candleholders... hang a fancy piece of gingerbread trim as a bath·tub/shower valance! Make a shelf from ancient moldings to display your treasures and photos... now,

aren't you clever?

Kitchenware Wind Chimes

Turn a Hodgepodge of Old Kitchenware into a melodious musical porch chime!

Here's what you need:

Tarnished silver-plate teapots, sugar bowls & creamers

Flour sifters

Tin measuring cups & spoons

Old mismatched silverware, including serving pieces, iced tea spoons, children's utensils

Mallet

Board for pounding on

Electric drill w/bits

Heavyweight nylon fishing line

How To:

1. Using the mallet & board, pound all forks & spoons flat.

2. Drill a small hole in silverware handles.

3. Drill small holes in bottom or around base of the large kitchen item that is the "main focus" of the chime. Drill holes opposite each other for balance in hanging.

4. Thread nylon line through holes on silverware handles & through hole in bottom of central large item ~ knot lines. A large serving spoon should hang in the center.

5. Thread line through top hole in central item to make a hanger. Enjoy!

I want one of those!

11

MARY ELIZABETH'S DIRTY LITTLE SECRET:

I can't resist An old hankie!

All right, I admit it. I can't walk away from a box-full of vintage hankies. Actually, any old fabric towel, quilt-top, feed sack makes my heart race and my face flush. I have drawers full. And closets full. And a basement full. Okay, I have 7214 old hankies, if you must know. And some day, I will put them all to good use.

I have big plans for them...

I'm gonna:

...Sew my hankies together into a duvet Cover & dust ruffle.

...make a hankie curtain from my sheerest & prettiest.

...make simple pillows, using hankies for the front & back. (I can make thousands!)

...sew 'em on all my jumpers for big pockets with personality.

...wrap up little gifts inside a beautiful hankie and tie it with a gorgeous satin ribbon.

...frame the prettiest ones so I can look at them everyday.

...Someday.

Make no little plans, they have no magic to stir men's blood. Make big plans, aim high in hope and work and let your watchword be order and your beacon beauty. - DAVID BURNHAM

Keepsakes
from the dresser Drawers

What to do with that collection of unstrung beads in the bottom of the jewelry box? The dozens of pairs of dainty white gloves folded neatly in the top drawer on the left? The Country Friends® have a few ideas up their sleeves on what you can do with those enigmatic treasures you've been hanging on to for sentimental reasons.

Oh better than the minting
Of a gold-crowned king
Is the safe-kept memory
Of a lovely thing.

— Sara Teasdale

14

"I Remember" Pots

Remember how your Grandma always wore those bright blue beads to church every Sunday? If you've inherited a box-full of costume jewelry from someone dear to you, put it to good use where you can see it every single day! Dig all the odds & ends out of your hiding place; hotglue the beads, chains, buttons & broken brooches to something practical you'll use or appreciate every day —

♥ A CLAY POT TO HOLD PENCILS BY THE PHONE

♥ A CLEAR LUCITE FRAME WITH A FAMILY PHOTO INSIDE

♥ A WOODEN BOX TO KEEP TREASURES IN BY THE BED

Every time you look at your handiwork, you'll think of someone you love.

Glove Love

Did Auntie Edna leave you a stack of lovely gloves from by-gone days? Enjoy them:

♥ FILL WITH FRAGRANT POTPOURRI & STITCH SHUT FOR A LOVELY SACHET.

♥ SEW A PAIR TO A PRETTY PILLOW FOR THE BOUDOIR. (THIS IS A THOUGHTFUL IDEA FOR USING A FLOWER GIRL'S TINY GLOVES AFTER THE WEDDING — a wonderful keepsake)

♥ WRAP AN ANTIQUE BROOCH IN TISSUE, SLIP INSIDE A GLOVE & TIE IT SHUT WITH A CHIFFON RIBBON... a nice way to pass on heirloom jewelry.

15

Cherished Children's Clothing

Just can't bear to give away those darling little dresses? That very-favorite-but-raggedy shirt your baby son wore everyday 'til he outgrew it? Pack away those precious memories or:

★ DRESS A DOLLY OR SPECIAL TEDDY WITH BABY'S CLOTHING.

★ HANG A VARIETY OF BABY THINGS — LITTLE SHIRTS, SOCKS, THOSE TINY SHOES! — ON A CLOTHESLINE IN YOUR LAUNDRY ROOM ... SWEET MEMORIES WILL MAKE YOU SMILE EVERY TIME YOU DO CHORES.

★ BEYOND-SAVING WORN-OUT & TIRED CLOTHING CAN STILL BE A MEMORY-MAKER: SNIP SALVAGABLE SECTIONS FROM KIDS' OLD CLOTHES. SAVE FABRIC UNTIL YOU HAVE ENOUGH SMALL PIECES TO MAKE A QUILT OR WALLHANGING.

Assorted Linens by the ton

Are you a packrat when it comes to vintage pillowcases, lovely embroidered towels and funky old fabrics? Turn 'em into decorating details ~ they're darling!

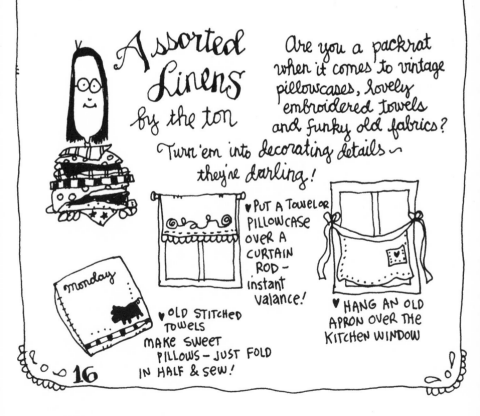

♥ PUT A TOWEL OR PILLOWCASE OVER A CURTAIN ROD — instant valance!

♥ OLD STITCHED TOWELS MAKE SWEET PILLOWS — JUST FOLD IN HALF & SEW!

♥ HANG AN OLD APRON OVER THE KITCHEN WINDOW

monday

A popsicle stick project

for Kids young & old

1. Collect the **p**opsicle **S**ticks.

(You may have to eat some ; it's a dirty job but someBody's goTTA get rid of the edible part)

2. Color the sticks with paints or crayons.

3. Glue the sticks together, overlapping the ends. If you're using hot glue, make sure an adult helps you.

4. When the frame is dry, decorate it by glueing something fun in the corners ⁓ a charm, old buttons, even a photo of you, cut-out ! Then put your favorite picture inside.

What Lurks in Gram's Cellar?

Interesting JARS

can be salvaged for a myriad of uses! Use as canisters in the bathroom for bathsalts & cotton balls... Wrap a heavy-weight wire around the rim and bend into a bail, then fill with an inch or so of sand for an imaginative patio candleholder... _neat_!

Old Luggage

...can be stacked and used as a unique side table by your bed. Paint 'em, decoupage 'em or use 'em as is!

Metal Tool Boxes look fine with a fresh coat of paint, or simply steel wool the old finish. Use them on your desk to hold supplies — a clever organizer!

Dust off old Bottles & Tin Cans to find intrigueing vases under the dirt!

Long-forgotten Keys can make striking jewelry; hang on a simple chain around your neck.

Vintage Dress Forms make interesting "sculpture" — paint & decorate with bright colors!

Real Treasures!

Reclaim an Old Trunk as a Dress-Up Kit for the little girl in your family.

OLD JARS

Other Great Basement Bargains

going down!

There's a wealth of ideas in those old books and encyclopedias! Tear or cut out maps, illustrations, botanicals and whatever else strikes your fancy... They make interesting

GIFTWRAP
WALLPAPER
* DECOUPAGE MATERIAL FOR OLD BOXES & TRUNKS *

Wooden ladders can have a new life ... prop against the wall for a towel hanger... hang one parallel to the ceiling on sturdy hooks for a primitive pot-rack.

Ideas are the root of creation. ~ ERNEST DIMNIT

OLD TOYS

JEANS

Turn a $10 sofa into a priceless **masterpiece** of **PAINTED UPHOLSTERY**

YOU'LL NEED:

* an old couch or chair
* acrylic paints mixed with a fabric medium or soft-to-the-touch fabric paints
* large soft paintbrushes

IT'S EASY!

1. Start painting on the back first to try out your design. Do your own thing or follow the fabric pattern. THINK BIG — no puny little designs. 2. Plan on finishing in one day — your painting style might change.

HEY! There's all kinds of GOOD junk down here!

THE BUGS

JUNK 1968

BOOKS

OH NO CHIPPED CHINA!

Don't pass up nicked & chipped plates & cups!

With a bit of imagineering, you can turn them into *wonderful works of art!*

Here are the tools you need:

- china plates & cups
- tile cutters
- small rubber mallet
- old towels
- tile adhesive or exterior construction adhesive
- tile grout, white or a color
- exterior sealer

HOW TO:

1. Place china between a towel and break it into good-sized pieces with your trusty mallet.
   Use tile cutters if smaller, more precise shapes are needed to make a design.

2. Use adhesive to adhere the broken pieces to:

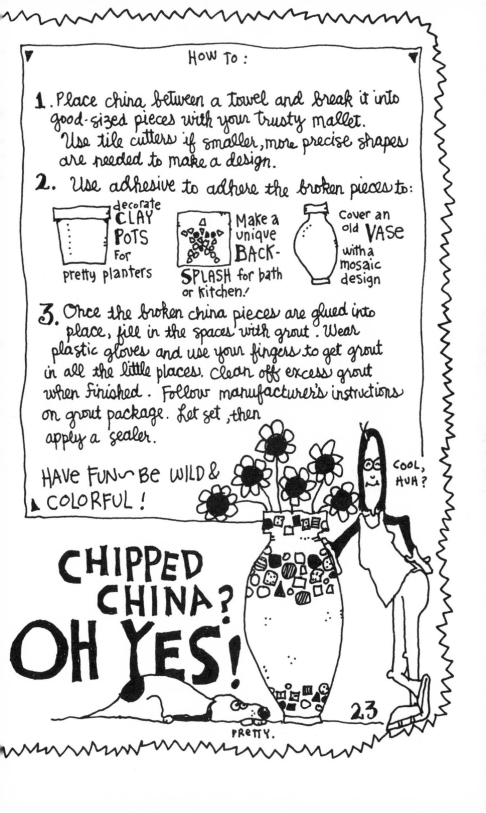

decorate CLAY POTS For pretty planters

Make a unique BACK-SPLASH for bath or kitchen!

Cover an old VASE with a mosaic design

3. Once the broken china pieces are glued into place, fill in the spaces with grout. Wear plastic gloves and use your fingers to get grout in all the little places. Clean off excess grout when finished. Follow manufacturer's instructions on grout package. Let set, then apply a sealer.

HAVE FUN ~ BE WILD & COLORFUL!

COOL, HUH?

CHIPPED CHINA?
OH YES!

PRETTY.

23

A CHIPPED CHINA PROJECT:

Mosaic
Country
Table·Top

How To:

It's easy! Just follow the guidelines on the previous page, but plan ahead a bit on this project as you're going to follow a design for your tabletop.

Find an unfinished wood or plywood circle or square that you can mount on something else to make a table. Kate used an old round patio table for her project, and cut a plywood "round" to fit the top. (* Be sure your choice is pretty sturdy as the new top will be kind of heavy.)

Learning is either a continuing thing or it is nothing.
-Frank Tyger-

First things first: Kate chose a primitive star for her design, so she pencilled it free-hand on the plywood, right in the middle.

She decided her star would be the "colorful" part of her design, and as she broke her china into small pieces, she separated the red & blue pieces into a distinct pile. (As you break your china, it is helpful to keep that idea in mind.)

Now, here's the

FUN PART:

Kate glued her "tiles" on, starting on the star, and once that was done, laid in all the white china bits around the star. She didn't quite stay in the lines, and one or two of the star's arms bend a little, but that's ok ∽ this was a country primitive project. (Just repeat that over & over as you work on yours.)

When your "tile" is all glued into place, finish up just like the directions on page 23 ∽ grout & clean up, let set as directed & seal... Kate mounted her mosaic on the old patio table, ran up the flag and enjoyed her project...

...now it's your turn!

We're afraid Holly is in serious danger of

Collection Overload...

She just can't leave those teacups alone!

So here are a few ideas for gift~giving that will help Holly thin out her collection...

and you know, of course, exactly what that means...

She can hunt for more!

Too many tea cups!

Remember that dainty little teacup you found at the neighbor's tag sale? It will make a thoughtful gift when you place a hand-full of teabags inside with this note.➡

Here's a gift from me to you... tea for a facial & a cup to drink, too!

Steaming Teatime Facial

Place 1 chamomile & 1 peppermint tea bag in a large pot. Add boiling water—allow to cool 2 minutes. Put a towel over your head & bowl & enjoy the refreshing steam!

Gather a square of tulle up around your teacup gift and tie at the top with a wide satin ribbon... it's all ready to deliver!

Potent Mint Potpourri

Stir up a batch of this fragrant concoction and package it in thrift shop tea cups... perfect little gifts.

Use a teacup:

♥ to hold cottonballs in the bathroom, or a guest soap by the sink

♥ as a sugarbowl when you have tea

♥ as a tealight or votive candleholder at each place setting at a dinner party or luncheon

♥ to keep paperclips & pins handy at a desk

½ c. orris root
1 T. oil of lavender
2 c. dried spearmint
2 c. dried peppermint
2 c. dried thyme leaves
1 c. dried rosemary

Combine orris root & oil. Add dried ingredients & mix gently – try not to crush leaves! Store in covered jar until you're ready to package it and give.

27

the Country Friends® Trash to Treasure
inspirations...

* For an instant vase: pop a bouquet in any can or jar. Gather a plaid kitchen towel up around the jar and tie near the mouth of the container with jute or ribbon.

* Doesn't everyone have a stack of raggedy bath towels? Cut 'em up and cover a pillow form ~ perfect, washable pillows for the deck!

* Turn boring old clay pots into pretty hanging vessels: simply drill 3 holes in the top with a high-speed drill (wear your goggles, please!), insert wire, twist wires together... and hang!

* Old glass milk bottles make interesting serving pieces at the table- try 'em with syrup!

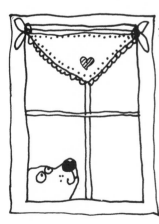

* Knot an antique hanky on the ends of a curtain rod to soften the edges. Pretty!

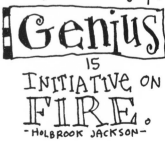

Genius
15
INITIATIVE ON
FIRE.
-HOLBROOK JACKSON-

Creative & impulses

* On a lonely old chair: decoupage a black & white copy of a family photo — granny's baby picture, perhaps? — on it for a piece you'll treasure forever.

* Put a pair of old painted shutters on either side of a mirror; pull a table & chair up for a quick country vanity.

* Don't pass up those plain white napkins & damask towels at the next tag sale— buy 'em, trace a cookie-cutter design on each one, then stitch along the line with bright red thread in an easy running stitch. Voilá! Neat embroidered napkins for the table!

* Scour sales for loose beads & charms — string them on raffia for simple & charming napkin rings!

Genius is 1% inspiration and 99% perspiration.
— THOMAS EDISON —

29

...Odds & ends...

* Make a POSY PIN from a vintage silver table knife! Simply use a saw to cut the knife handle to the desired length ⌒ about 2" to 2½".
  Glue a jewelry pinback onto the backside, and fill the hollow knife handle with fresh flowers. (* to keep your petite bouquet fresh, poke a moistened cottonball down inside the handle.)

* Too lazy to refinish that kitchen table? Cover the worn top with a 40's tablecloth, then lay on a glass top to protect the colorful cloth... cheery & easy to clean.

Genius
is only a Superior way of seeing. – JOHN RUSKIN

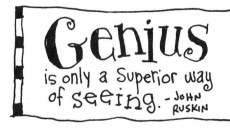

* Put old silverware to work as clever cabinet & drawer pulls: just drill through them with a 5/32 metal bit... attach a small wooden spool (available at craft stores) behind the piece with epoxy glue to act as a "spacer"... then screw through the spoon and spacer into the door or drawer.

30

* Kitchen chairs don't match? Paint 'em all the same base color, then give every member of the family a paintbrush & turn 'em loose! Squiggles, hearts, plaids ⌒ everybody paints their own chair for a personalized seating arrangement. Can you say "PICASSO"?

★ Dye a crummy old basket a pretty color... Just mix a packet of dye in an old tub, following packet directions. Wear rubber gloves & dip basket into the dye, constantly moving & rotating it. Remove from dye bath & dry it on several layers of newspaper over a sheet of plastic. When dry, add decorative hand-painted ants, stars or flowers on each strip... a wonderful picnic basket idea!

and...

★ Collect mismatched china & odds-and-ends glasses & mugs to put together a personality-packed picnic set. Things just taste better off pretty plates!

Everyone Loves a bargain.

to make the common marvelous is the test of a Genius.

—James Russell Lowell—

31